Wolf Hill

The Night it Rained Chips

Roderick Hunt

Illustrated by Alex Brychta

OXFORD
UNIVERSITY PRESS

OXFORD

UNIVERSITY PRESS

Great Clarendon Street, Oxford, OX2 6DP

Oxford   New York
Athens   Auckland   Bangkok   Bogota   Buenos Aires   Calcutta
Cape Town   Chennai   Dar es Salaam   Delhi   Florence   Hong Kong
Istanbul   Karachi   Kuala Lumpur   Madrid   Melbourne   Mexico City
Mumbai   Nairobi   Paris   São Paulo   Singapore   Taipei   Tokyo
Toronto   Warsaw

and associated companies in
Berlin   Ibadan

Oxford is a trade mark of Oxford University Press

© text Roderick Hunt 1998
© illustrations Alex Brychta
First Published 1998
Reprinted 1999

ISBN 019 918659 6

Printed in Hong Kong

Chapter 1

Chris couldn't believe it. The school gate was blocked up. He couldn't get in.

Chris ran round to the front of the school. 'I'm going to be late,' he thought.

He wasn't late but something odd
was going on. Children were
standing outside the main gate.
Chris could hear laughing.

Chris saw Kat and Gizmo. 'What's
going on?' he asked.

Kat grinned. 'We've got to keep out.' She pointed to a big new notice. It said:

'But that doesn't mean us,' said Chris.

'No,' said Gizmo, 'but you know what day it is? It's April 1st. It's a good joke.'

Some of the adults had joined in the joke.

'I wonder what Mr Saffrey will do,' said Gizmo.

'We'll soon see,' said Kat. 'Here he comes.'

Chapter 2

Mr Saffrey came to the gate. 'Why haven't you come in?' he called.

'We can't,' said Michael Ward. 'Have you seen that notice? It says "Keep out".'

The notice was new. It had been put up at the weekend. Mr Saffrey looked at it and then he laughed.

'It's our smart notice board,' he said. 'But it's not as smart as you.'

'It's a good April Fool's joke,' went on Mr Saffrey. 'Now, let's go in.'

Everyone laughed. They began to push through the gate.

As Mr Saffrey shut the gate, a huge truck stopped.

The driver called out, 'I've got a delivery for Wolf Hill School.'

'A delivery of what?' said Mr Saffrey.

'Chips,' said the man. 'Two tonnes of chips.'

Mr Saffrey groaned. 'It's April 1st,' he said. 'Is this another joke?'

Chapter 3

It wasn't a joke. The truck was full of wood chips for the adventure playground.

The adventure playground was new. The children had helped design it. So far nobody had used it. They couldn't - not until the wood chips had been put down.

'What are the chips for?' asked Andy.

'You know,' said Najma. 'They go on the ground.'

'But why?' asked Andy.

'For safety,' said Gizmo. 'In case anyone falls. The chips make a soft landing.'

Everyone watched the huge truck. It was backing through the gate.

'It's a big truck for a few wood chips,' said Loz.

They heard Mr Saffrey shout. 'Come on!' he called.

'I don't think the truck will make it,' said Gizmo. 'The gate is too narrow.'

Chapter 4

Everyone sat in the hall. Mr Saffrey smiled. He had long bony fingers. He made them click.

'I wish he wouldn't click like that,' said Kat. 'It means he's up to something.'

'I have good news and bad news,' said Mr Saffrey. 'This is the good news. The adventure playground is almost ready.'

Everyone cheered, but Mr Saffrey
held up his hand.

'The bad news is that we still can't
use it. The truck with the wood
chips can't get through the gate.'

Everyone groaned. 'Never mind,' said Mr Saffrey. 'I've asked the driver to dump the wood chips in the gateway. I want you to shift them to the adventure playground.'

'I told you he was up to something,' said Kat.

Chapter 5

Mr Saffrey was in for a shock. The pile of wood chips was enormous. It looked like a small mountain. It covered the gate posts. It spilled into the playground.

The truck had gone.

'How can anyone get through the gate?' said Loz. 'It's blocked by a chip mountain.'

Mr Saffrey gulped. 'Right everyone,' he said. 'The wood chips are quite dry. Carry them over to the adventure playground.'

The children had their plastic trays. They started to fill the trays with big handfuls of chips. Then they carried them across the playground.

'That's good,' said Mr Saffrey.
'We'll soon shift them.'

Mr Saffrey was wrong. Shifting the
wood chip mountain wasn't easy.
Things didn't go as Mr Saffrey had
planned.

Chapter 6

The chips were light to carry but some of them spilled on to the ground.

The smaller children found it even harder. Some of them dropped their trays. Soon there were wood chips all over the playground.

The wood chip mountain was as big as ever.

'The wood chips are dusty,' said Miss Teal. 'It's starting to rain. The children are getting filthy. The parents won't be pleased,'

'Oh dear!' said Mr Saffrey. 'This wasn't one of my best ideas.'

A man appeared on top of the pile of chips. 'You'll have to do something,' he said. 'Both gates are blocked. No one can get into the school.'

Mr Saffrey sighed. 'No one can get out either,' he said, 'and it's almost time to go home.'

Chapter 7

Mr Saffrey went to his office. He wrote a letter to the families. He asked them to help move the wood chips.

The teachers gave the letters to the children.

'I hope the parents won't think this is a joke,' said Mr Saffrey. 'It is April 1st.'

'They won't when they see how dirty the children are,' said Miss Teal.

It was time to go home. The adults began to arrive. They looked at the pile of wood chips blocking the gate.

Some of them began to grumble.

'I'm sorry,' said Mr Saffrey. 'The children will just have to climb over.'

One parent pointed to the new sign. 'It says "Keep out",' he said, 'but this is ridiculous.'

'I'm glad it's Friday,' said Miss Teal.

Chapter 8

Mr Saffrey went home late. He looked glumly at the pile of wood chips.

'I wish I could wave a magic wand,' he thought, 'and by tomorrow they'd all be gone.'

A wind began to blow. It blew some of the wood chips along the ground.

The sky looked inky black. The weather vane on the school roof swung from side to side.

'It looks like bad weather,' thought Mr Saffrey.

He was right. That night there was a terrible storm.

The wind beat against the houses. It blew tiles off roofs. It tore branches off trees. People stayed indoors.

The wind slapped round the chip mountain. It began to blow the wood chips up into the air. First a few flew up. Then more and more. It was the night it rained chips.

Chapter 9

The wind was like a giant vacuum cleaner. It sucked up the wood chips. They rose up like a cloud. They spun madly in the air. Higher and higher they went.

The wood chips blew all over the town. They landed in the streets. They landed on roofs and in gardens.

The storm lasted all night.

The next day some of the parents turned up to help move the wood chips.

Loz and her Gran walked up Wolf
Street. Gran had her wheelbarrow.
Loz had a big box. 'That's funny,'
said Gran. 'There are wood chips
everywhere.'

Mr Saffrey was looking at the school gate.

As for the chip mountain - it had disappeared.

'I made a silly wish,' said Mr Saffrey. 'I didn't think it would come true.'